CW00402820

Index:

Chapter <u>One</u>:
Tributes

"Throughout life we all pay tribute to those who have touched us the most."- Joshua West

Death of a Metalhead

A friendship forged at a live show
Headbanging, standing side by side
Passing knowledge to who would know
Getting all involved in the musical tide

Friendship strengthened in the mosh pit
Rushing in the wall of death it was solidified
Heard news that stole my laugh, I didn't believe it
Day darkened when I heard that you died

Our community was rocked by that news
A hole left that no one could ever fill
But it is a sad fact that none can refuse
You have now left the world standing still

Life got involved and gave you a release
You are gone but your love of music will stay
So my brother in metal, rest in peace
Goodbye Tom, we will meet up again one day.
©Josh West

Tribute to Alexi Laiho
08/04/1979 - 29/12/2020

A day stricken with a black mark
On this day a brother fell
A lightless shadow, eternal dark
It can be heard through the tolling bell

The sadness spread across our scene
Taken so soon, the world is now on pause
The hole left in the metal world forever to be seen
Will anyone take up your musical cause?

Rest in peace my brother
You may be gone, we will not forget
Because like you there will never be another
Your music inspired millions, we will never forget.
©Josh West

A Letter to the Fallen
Dedicated to the memory of Lance Corporal Michael
West
1892-1918 aged 26.

You heard your country's call
You stood before the flag and gave an oath
For country and family, you honour them both
Take up arms and carry them to the fall

Stand upon a battlefield so vast
Obeying the command of those in charge
Facing the unknown, a burden so large
Hearing the snap and hiss of rounds flying past

The screams of pain as bullets strike their mark
The sounds of those next to you hitting the ground
In the dying hours of the dark, you hear the sound
The next one is yours, sent by a firearms bark

Some make it back fine, others as broken souls
Many don't come back at all, this is for them
They gave the greatest sacrifice, remember them
They guard still, standing by countless holes

If they passed on fighting or peacefully asleep
They are still veterans, they will not be forgot
Honour them, if they died in bed or got shot
Honour them for your safety they tried to keep.
©Josh West

Chapter <u>Two</u>:
Views of the World.

"How the world is seen is dictated by the mind of the
individual and circumstances faced"- Joshua West

The Controlled

Upon this field of death and victory
Placed there to get the job done
Body counts rise, the same story rerun
Hands of the mighty control the story

The puppet masters pull the strings
"Go there, do that" the stringed lead the way
At the end, the controlled are the ones to pay
Puppets controlled by those toting burnt wings

The master's hands controlled by another power
A stronger beast infused with barbaric intent
Power so great that to its will all others are bent
Controlling all minds from an unseen tower.
©Josh West

Man in a Maze

In a mental prison painted white
Eyes dazzled by shining light
Sun seems to shine at night
Reflecting from everywhere, light so bright
Sun shining night and day, something's not right

Like a blind man in a maze
Counting out the final days
Looking out through a haze
In a self-induced chemical daze
Flaws exposed by a trying phase

Breathing air now decades stale
Experimented on for being a male
Here for so long skin has turned pale
Blood-stained footprints leave a trail
Now ended with a skull piercing nail.
©Josh West

Honouring the Left-Handed

For centuries, seen as bad
Changes forced upon the young
Left hand punished, teacher glad
For those forced to change it's the saddest song sung

Now lefties are accepted by society
But there is still a long way to go
The changes are slow and hard to see
Still seen as weird by those who don't know

Instruments are hard to find
Some tools are hard to use
Lefties have a secret that together they bind
Lefties are no longer a joke to amuse

Together they are part of a whole
The few amongst the population
They stand united like fish in a shoal
It is time to reveal this revolution

It is time to rise up and take a stand
For the longest time the left-handed were seen as lesser
beings
Show them there is nothing wrong with using the left
hand
Show the world we are the kings and queens.
©Josh West

Slave to the World

Clouds of the darkest hue
Across the horizon are rolling
The sign of storms I am due
A time of life with no consoling

The world filled with muted shades
Standing, staring into the storm's eye
One foot in hope, the other where all fades
Is there place here for the likes of I?

Rudimentary thought fills my aching head
Truth denied by a single ironclad wing
Force my mouth open, fill it with molten lead
Hand me a noose of words, watch me swing

Robbed of thought, my voice has been taken
Essence of the individual, erased by a brute
Deprived of choice, a sign not to be mistaken
A slave to the world, thoughtless and mute.
©Josh West

Ways of the World

I sit in silence
Just listening to the world
Weeping at the daily violence
Wishing I could just lay in a ball tightly curled

Daily mutterings of bloodshed
Thickening the airways like glue
People eager to fill others with lead
It seems to have started out of the blue

Bodies get piled higher and higher
Soil soaked with a river of thick blood
Families left to put out the growing fire
Tears of those left behind flow in a tidal flood

Trying to prove who can be more vicious
Locked in a cycle, the wheel turns
The world run by the truly malicious
Where their fingers point, humanity burns

These are the ways of the world
Where the cruel will rise
The weak get crushed, lives unfurled
Ways of the world? Planets demise.
©Josh West

Chapter Three:
Trails of Life

"Life is what you make it? No, sometimes it will let you win, but most times it exists only to break you down."-
Joshua West

Game of Life

Life, a game won by none
Born with an expiry date
Living to die, what great fun
Conquest of life, death begun
Death, the final card, there's no debate

The game of life designed to tease
A tempting cycle, there will be no ease
Birth and death, daybreak and nightfall
A chilling tale of finality, hearts will seize
No use trying to escape it, death will have all

The bells toll, the sound signals a change
Life flashes past on this downward heading road
The virulent infection of life lives by a code
Leading to a land where the demons strode
A land of desolation where the living can't range

The game of life, where no one will ever win
Here on the edge, reality has grown thin
Born into wealth or a pauper, all die the same
In love or broken hearted, climb into life's bin
Damnation is the only thing life has ever given.
©Josh West

Failure

Failure is said to be the greatest teacher
But the only thing I have is a bitter taste
I am left feeling like the lowest creature
Fail after fail, one more time waste

A new attempt and one more fail
Should I even bother trying again?
Constant failure ever present, this is now stale
Do I have a fail needle stuck in a vein?

One more failed effort and I will break
Anything new has become a pointless task
Should I even try again knowing what is at stake?
My disappointing failures now cover my face like a mask

Right now giving up seems the safest bet
Every single fail has turned my heartbeat sour
Surrounded by hourly failure I always fret
It seems that all I can do is hide my face and cower.
©Josh West

Reforged

Simple thought laced with complex emotion
Lost in the hand drawn pictures my mind conjured
While trying to withstand every childish compulsion
Changes are coming, will my core escape uninjured?

Urges to pull myself down and ruin what others helped
build
Listening daily to two beings, each so unlike the other
Am I doomed to be torn in two or will one be stilled?
My worry is will the stilled be replaced with another?

Like a boat that from the shore has come untethered
I am just floating, aimlessly drifting
I must trust my heart, though it's aging and weathered
But will I survive when the sands of memory start
shifting?

A voice heard cutting through, drowning out the trouble
Who, what is it? A person or angelic being?
I was pulled away as the ground began to boil and
bubble
Saved from myself, can spoken words be this freeing?

Now standing reforged, a book with blank pages
Facing the joy of life driven by my heart
My tale is unknown to all but the ancient sages
Can I make my story worthy of the new start?
©Josh West

Guilt

Lost within a prison cell of torment
As the guilt is sitting deep in my mind
Just sitting, festering inside my heart

My fallen tears bear the scent of shame
I will have to hurt myself as much as I can
I am left with no choice, I must cheer up

I will have to hurt myself now
I have this need to find my release
It is now time to punish myself for this

Taking my time choosing my toy of bloodshed
I will show just what this guilt looks like
My blood stained body will be seen by all

Powerful words turned into a verbal spike
Nothing I can do will rip those words away
My fractured mentality has paid the price

Like maggots on a corpse, the guilt crawls
I will destroy myself to remove this feeling
I surrender all I am to end how I feel.
©Josh West

Penance?

Wrapped in life's coldest embrace
Waking up to life's middle finger
The raised finger pressed to my face
As fragmenting dreams I always chase
What is the point now, why should I linger?

In the cross-fire of abuse, hatred gleams
Addicted to being a beating post for others
Ears bleeding from the relentless screams
Lines of fire mark me in cross-stitched seams
Why am I the only one life always smothers?

The punching bag for life I have become
Cold distress as life pushes in sadistic pins
Desensitized to the treatment, growing numb
Gouging out my eyes with a mangled thumb
Is this penance for my growing list of sins?
©Josh West

Fighting Negativity

Thoughts swirling, blocking the light
Tightening grip, breaking clarity
Paralyzing fear, eyes devoid of sight
Negativity sets in, stealing charity

Mind-set dialled to self-defeat
Nothing done will ever be good enough
My safe place, to the negative I retreat
It always whispers, showing life as rough

Saying to quit, just give it up now
That nothing good can be done
Purpose slowing, shutting down somehow
Is this it? Has negativity really won?

Well-meant compliments go unheard
Positivity set back whilst self-breaking
Setting up a swan dive into the absurd
Fighting the negative, no more faking

One step, then another, the mist lifting
Fighting for control, opposites at war
Through combat, tides are shifting
Conflict crashing the line of the shore.
©Josh West

Torment

Dragging myself from one day to the next
Ideas turn stagnant even when newly formed
Unable to sleep, walls covered with strange red text
Hiding it from others, they must stay uninformed

Before I go out, my mask must smile
The mask I wear in order to hide my tears
I must act happy while self-loathing rises like bile
Breaking under the strain is the greatest of my fears

No one must see that I am slowly dying inside
Despite my best efforts, you see pain in my eyes
I need some help but am too ashamed to confide
When you see me, turn away from my voiceless cries

With each day I become less than I was the day before
There is something inside me slicing like a knife
I am giving up, leave me be, let me stay huddled on the floor
The darkness has taken everything, now I give it my life.
©Josh West

Heart on Fire

People always want to get close
But I'm too scared to let them in
When my name is called, I want another dose
To disappear and live with my joyful sin

I'm scared of the happiness they own
When my brightest day is as dark as night
I am burnt by the love they have shown
The fire is lit but I see no light

I hide who I am behind all my rage
Call me a coward, I won't stop you
For most of my life I have kept my heart in a cage
There were always people around but I never knew

I am faceless, one of the unknown
My only friend is pure dark hate
I put everyone I see onto a throne
It seems that is doomed to be my fate

Please burn me with that fire
Because I have never felt any pain
Don't even dare call me a liar
The truth is I am just insane

I have been in the dark for too long
There is no one to save me from my trouble
Just block out my cries with another song
Carry on living your perfect life in your tiny bubble

There is nothing more for me to learn
So I will just stand and study every face
All I can do is just wait for my turn
And control things at my own pace

When I am seen, everyone tries to hide
As if they are scared that I am going to bite
I look at them and they look off to the side
Can't they see I have no desire to fight?

I hate the person I have become
I am tired of people fearing me
I just want love but no one will give me some
To slay the monster and set me free

Every day I have to force a smile
Have to pretend that I care
My life is just another page in a file
There is nothing left for me anywhere

I live in my very own piece of hell
I wish I could spread my wings and fly away
To escape before I fall under another spell
Before I am seen and forced to stay

It feels like I am blind
I look around and see nothing that makes me happy
Nothing to make my body and soul bind
This just might be the end of me

All I ever wanted was to make you proud
All I ever needed was to feel your love
©Josh West

Betting Life

Sitting in the smoky room of my mind
Across the table my opponent stares
Eyes intense like beasts in their lairs
Trying to read each other in kind
Ignoring all the unspoken dares

On the table the game goes on
Playing a game of poker with life
While death deals the cards of strife
Playing a stacked deck, hope is gone
The stakes being my sharpest knife

Losing is possible but winning is not
Hand after hand, losing every match
It is my living force life wants to dispatch
In the grin of death it wants me to rot
My life for my death is this game's catch

Life and death are one, they are the same
Scars of life mean one foot in the grave
Bound to death as life's toy, I am the slave
They have taken all including my name
I have lost the game of all to life, the knave.
©Josh West

<u>Chapter</u> <u>Four</u>:
Self-Reflection

"No one judges harder than us when we stare and search deep within ourselves."- Joshua West

Duality

Pushed away but held in place
And pulled deep within myself
Phantom hands pawing at my face
I want to both stay and run and hide from myself
Could I heal my fractured mentality with some lace?

Living life down on my broken knees
Head low, face down never looking out
While my heart, torment will surely squeeze
Each piece of me gives voice to an anguished shout
Will I be free even if the torments cease?

Hands clutch my head tight so it won't burst
I can't take any more of this fight
I feel like I am dying of unquenchable thirst
Eyes wide but the shade robbed me of sight
Reflections, my duality, but which me was first?
©Josh West

Humanities Mask

Surrounded by and drowning in humanities crowd
Feeling physically sick from their stink
Deafened by their babble, spoken so loud
Senses overwhelmed by people, I cannot think

Trying to avoid the curious stares
Trying to ignore all fingers pointed
While being stung by angry glares
With the disgust of the unfriendly, I am anointed

To ensure my loathing can't be seen, I hide my face
Ears and nose blocked to try to remain pure
I must keep my mask on to blend in with the human race
For I am an ungodly, hideous beast that has no cure

At times my mask slips and my revolting face is shown
When it happens, they stare and point at the disgusting
freak
Making me wish that out of my ears, my brain could be
blown
That way I could fit in with the masses when they speak

Forced to live in a world where I don't belong
I will just have to make due, no matter how unfair
I must keep this thing on the rest of my life's sad song
This is humanities mask that I am forced to wear.
©Josh West

Idiot

The eternal idiot that is me
Letting mindless words escape
From my flapping mouth, they break free
I rebuke my idiot self, beaten to another shape

I need to think before speaking
Always making others uncomfortable when I talk
I should break my jaw to stop my attention seeking
Or rip out my pathetic tongue so no words can walk

Hating myself when using words without thought
Cursing myself as a fool, just an idiot
I should check if wisdom can be store bought
Why am I such a stupid idiot?
©Josh West

The Superhero

I wear no costume but am a hero
I am a superhero without a cape
Look for me when life hits zero
Your suffering is covered with a drape

In a moment of weakened emotion
A razor blade became your best friend
Sawing back and forth, comforting motion
It is becoming an addictive trend

I know what you are feeling
I see the blood that is drying
I know the joy that life keeps stealing
I can hear your nightly crying

Take my hand, I will lead you away
I will save you from the dark
I will be your support in your darkest day
I will try to erase every razor's mark

Instead of wearing a mask
The scars of the world, I will wear
Others have fallen from this task
But I vow to you, I will be there

The razor wants to hurt, don't let it win
Even when in your mind, memories dredge
It wants to become your demise, it mustn't win
I want to save the world from a razor's edge.
©Josh West

Josh West: The Soundtrack

Not sure how to start this
My soundtrack is told by all who failed
In this telling, some crucial point I am sure to miss
Will getting something wrong get me jailed?

Sorry, not sorry, there, who cares?
Sneaking around, the attention I don't like
Leave me alone; let me finish eating your teddy bears
Once done, will you put me on stage and hand me a
mic?

My image is seen as serious but really just a clown
Always joking to brighten your day
In person you will see I seldom wear a frown
But why would I change in any way?

Making a fool of myself to amuse those I care about
A shy person, I use humour to hide my flaws
When following my passion I growl, scream and shout
Would you like to hear my voice when sharpened into
claws?

Story time is now over; I have said all I need
I truly hope that on your face, I made a smile crack
This is a small insight into the life I lead
Did you enjoy my very own soundtrack?
©Josh West

Lost Innocence

Sitting there a shade of who I used to be
Trying to figure out where it all went wrong
My innocence has gone, been doing it for so long
Eyes upon the course but I cannot see
Now just one more word in the cutters song

I opened that door, now I am afraid to close it
Reasons to do it, the lies my reflection told
Pretending I am fine, leave things untold
I caress myself with sand paper's roughest grit
Will I be able to break this dangerous mental hold?

Being pulled back into the addiction of pain
I know what I am tempting, what is at stake
I can't take anymore, giving into the break
Eyes closed, arms out, bloodied in my lane
I give up as madness on my body starts to rake.
©Josh West

Fire of Indecision

Doubt in myself leads the way
Insecurities carved in stone
Not sure of the truth in what others say
Thanking them for their care, their kindness unknown
Will I ever stop tearing myself down every day?

In my mind, thoughts always churn
Am I good enough? Will I ever be?
Maybe I should wait for fate to take another turn
Am I smart enough? Will I ever be?
The fire of indecision, am I going to burn?

Making choices is a chore, which way to go?
Afraid to choose, if I am wrong I can't restart like a game
Doubt, choices, chilling my blood and making my brain
slow
Picking wrong would be bad, if I don't, will I stay the
same?
Or will I be changed like a feather by a careless blow?

If right or wrong, will I survive?
My heart says yes, my brain strongly disagrees
If I go down, is there anyone who will revive?
All I want is to be truly me
But isn't that like taking a blindfolded, head first dive?

I know that feeling this makes me a coward
Each day facing the world feeling listless
Not ready to move when over me shadows have
towered
Afraid to move even though I am in a bath of souring
piss
How can I go on while feeling less empowered?

So if you see me in a corner weeping
I have a choice to make, please make my choice
Because through my eyes, my courage is leaking
So please choose and give my cowardice a voice
Will you stand by me when the choice starts reaping?
©Josh West

Hating Self

Hatred in my heart will deeply infest
No words can ease my rage, so vile
Left with a sour taste, like drinking bile
A dark entity inside, I am failing the test

A friend was in need, I couldn't aid
Feeling pathetic, I failed my friend
Try as I may, I couldn't help her mend
Will she accept any help or slowly fade?

My help is needed, too stupid to assist
Punishment! Punish! My heart cries
But in doing so a part of me slowly dies
Hopeless help given while my soul will resist

I want to help but don't know what she needs
I know she needs something to let her cope
But can I give it? Me, weak like worn out rope
Can I save her while I struggle in the reeds?

I failed her but I won't ask to be forgiven
I don't deserve forgiveness for not being there
Unable to give her comfort, compassion and care
So I will stay here being guilt driven.
©Josh West

The Fallen

Here I sit on my own
Body trembling as I try not to cry
Fate rising from deeds I have sown
What have I done? And why?

I look at myself daily and say
"Look at you, so fucking weak"
"Pathetic, unworthy, just go away"
Loathing reaching the climatic peak

Here I am, a shade of who I used to be
Once a pillar of strength for all to use
Now a vile creature. Yes, that is me
A broken, empty vessel. A burnt out fuse

I made my choice; I have the marks of mistakes
They linger like the scent of a putrid bathroom stall
I am a dire warning against a life without brakes
I am semi living proof that the mighty can fall.
©Josh West

Ocean

Adrift, lost at sea
Aimlessly floating
No safety can my eyes see
Open oceans heard gloating
At the mercy of the tidal flow
Will I be saved? I don't know

At the horizon I squint, I see a dot
A tiny speck, almost lost in the ocean
Trying to gauge how far, is this my only shot?
Will I be able to resist the tides pulling motion?
Watching intently, it never draws any nearer
A straight line, the objective couldn't be clearer

But do I swim and risk being drowned?
Or stay put and suffer with hope?
I must choose fast and to my path be bound
But with either choice will my aching body cope?
The chance of failure is almost too high
The truth is that doing any and I will probably die

Ever crashing waves threaten to drag all things under
Safety is my only thought as into the water I dive
Punished by crushing waves and their roaring thunder
Was I a fool for doing this? Will I survive?
The ocean is my own dark insanity
This is my struggle to reclaim the real me.
©Josh West

Faceless

On a journey through the unknown
A quest to finally become seen
Moving onward to the generic scene
Across time where altered futures are shown
To a land where truth and lies are grown

Walking in hopes of finding who I am
To discover my place in this land of fake
I need to find all the answers, for my own sake
A stalking deadly wolf or gentle little lamb
Will I be told or is it my choice to make?

Maybe I will finally find my very own face
An identity that I can really call mine
Or could I end up in a box made of pine?
Second guessing this as my mind starts to race
Still walking, trying to ignore my doubting sign

I hope I am able to complete this trying task
Doing this so I can live in my own little bubble
To stop being a disappointment bringing trouble
Because I am tired of wearing someone else's mask
For now I am faceless digging through the rubble.
©Josh West

Fading Shadow

My eyes are burning
Vision blurred with tears
Crippled by my lonesome fears
My world has stopped turning

Mouth torn wide, at the world I scream
Singing the chorus to heartbreak's song
Trying to understand what I did wrong
As I try to escape from life's broken dream

As my anguish is portrayed
Across my face, my fingers rake
Depression deepens, looking to break
Emotions dead, light delayed

Surrounded by muttering voices
This is my fault they whisper
The cold surety of it grows crisper
I know it was ruined by my choices

I have locked my heart in a cage
A broken soul, breaking even more
Guilt, grief, in my mind they bore
I remain loveless to my dying age

Through pages of my life, the ink ran
Thought gave birth to hope, hope lied
Suffering alone, I stand with the tears I cried
Just the fading shadow once a man.
©Josh West

Conversing With Myself

Standing before a mirror, staring deep
Clearing my mind, ignoring those around
Looking to find a hint that I can keep
Asking who I am as thought begins to seep
Looking for answers, will they be found?

The face in the mirror watches, taunting
I smile but my reflection returns a frown
The unknown in its gaze appears daunting
The glimmer of secrets those eyes keep flaunting
Two pairs of eyes lock, eyes the same shade of brown

My eyes staring back at me, seeming to gloat
Leaning in closer, my face drifting nearer
While in the back of my mind, thoughts float
A rare union of two sides, a harmonic note
Conversing with myself, eyes growing clearer

From two mouths the same voice is talking
Questions asked but no real answers being given
On a reflected landscape two halves are walking
The conversation goes on, oblivious to all the gawking
Along the winding path, to the answers I am driven

Answers hidden within a world slowly turned skew
Reflections twist as the duality starts to slack
Revelations promised inside a witches brew
I need to solve this riddle and find what is true
Am I the one staring or the one staring back?
©Josh West

Memoirs

Sitting alone as the darkness creeps
As through the tattered book of my life, I flip
Happiness faked with a grin full of teeth
This page, a fool giving up a lover's wreath
Memoirs of a wasted life studied with a quivering lip
From each page another forgotten memory leaps

Page after tear stained page, visual despair
Lines traced along this, my very own sad tale
Storm-laden heart looking, searching for a token
This page, a man on a journey for the broken
Raw emotional turbulence, hidden within a veil
Head grown heavy beneath depression's flare

Scenes etched on paper, revisiting childhood
Reliving the past, finding scars that time faded
Mental sounds from the past, so vociferant
This page, a small boy bullied for being different
I still smell the spit, feel the blows that cascaded
Didn't they see I tried to fit in the best I could?

Tears rubbed away using bloodied fingers
Hurting myself just to try numb the pain
The damage, the danger, rolling the dice of chance
This page, a teenager doing death's deadly dance
Doing all I can with no thought of refrain
While the scent of my torment still lingers

Sitting and wondering if I am truly alive
A victim of fate, hopes and wishes now scrapped
Trying not to drown in thought's rivers and streams
This page, a man who dared to have dreams
Surrounded by these memories, I am trapped
Struggling to breathe while just trying to survive

Learning to embrace my past, it can't be rewritten
Only then will my history and present blend
Accepting who I was, who I am, trying not to doubt
This page, a man busy writing all this out
Who knows how this will all come to an end
A story is only done when the last word is written.
©Josh West

Printed in Great Britain
by Amazon